MLM Prospecting fo

CW01095690

by Richard Williams

Table of Contents

Special Thanks

This book is dedicated to Marketing Excellence of Perry Marshall, Mike Dillard, Mark Wieser, Todd Falcone, Ray Higdon, David Wood, Robert Blackman & Tim Sales.

1

My Story

The first thing you should know before reading this book is I am not a millionaire.
I am not a PhD in network marketing.
I am not a network marketing guru or expert.
I am just an ordinary guy with kickass marketing skills that helps me to do a lot of things.

I have failed more times than I succeeded. I learnt many things the hard way. I tried several approaches which don't work, found out some which work through trial and error.

I tried some approaches which I thought would never work but worked fabulously and some approaches which I thought would work were severely bombed.

There are a lot of people running and claiming that they have all the answers. I don't proclaim that I have all the answers for you but whatever answers I have are pretty important.

You shouldn't just believe whatever I say, infect I suggest you to go through my material with healthy skepticism and scientific perspective and put the ideas to use and see for yourself how great they work.

This book <u>won't</u> make you successful or rich, thinking something outside yourself to make yourself successful is a pathetic approach.

Whatever you need to succeed is already in you. This book will only help you to acquire some new skills.

If you want to work on yourself, I will suggest you to get this book "**Psycho cybernetics**" by Dr. Maxwell Maltz

In this book, I will talk about all the approaches you can use but a small warning before you go through them.

<u>WARNING</u>: This book is not a be-all and end-all solution for Network Marketing. All the approaches I talk about <u>won't</u> work for everybody. There will be some approaches which would work absolutely great for you and some approaches would work terribly bad, that doesn't mean it's a useless approach. It just means that this approach is not suitable for you. It all depends upon your personality, your work ethics, your background, your work experience.

Now before I dive into the nitty gritty, I wanted to share a few things about myself which I believe you will find important.

First everyone sucks in the beginning, I did for long time and even my upline did, but many of them never bothered to mention it.

They just <u>casually forgot to go over that little piece of info,</u> and many of them never bothered to mention that.

I got started in this industry just after I lost my hope to get into good MBA college after <u>1 year of job and 1 year of failed attempt at MBA preparation.</u>

Exactly on my birthday, I was recruited by my closest friend. This was a massive, hugely uncomfortable stretch for me.

He tried to convince me for 1 year in vain but I didn't join it for some personal reasons as I wanted to try my luck at MBA which didn't yield any stellar results except few converts here and there.

Eventually, I signed up with him after he followed up with me for long time.

When I got started, I had very little self confidence and was close to dead broke. I used to drive my upline mad with endless questions and someone who would do whatever to avoid calling my prospects. Maybe you can relate.

But I "*saw the circles*" and grasped the potential, and my little world was greatly expanded as we travelled from my home to some very posh areas.

I hanged out with a lot of people from corporate, from traditional businesses and many more people like me, who believed that the future of the world lies in this powerful "new" concept of Network Marketing.

The short version of that story is that I was completely *'sold out'* or rather completely brainwashed , did whatever they told me to do, I bought whatever they told me to buy, I went to every small and big event possible and dug in deep till I went into debt. I couldn't attend some big events because I had very little or no money left with me.

Still I had the persistence of Saddam Hussein.

In a long span of 18 months, I travelled a couple hundred miles and did hundreds of presentations with my uplines and on my own.
In fact I even went through a dry spell where I got 126 NO's in a row.

No No No No No No No No No No No No No No No No No
No No No No No No No No No No No No No No No No No
No No No No No No No No No No No No No No No No No
No No No No No No No No No No No No No No No No No
No No No No No No No No No No No No No No No No No
No No No No No No No No No No No No No No No No No
No No No No No No No No No No No No No No No No No
No No No No No No No.

I know. It doesn't sound like much or it doesn't look that bad on paper but for me it felt like NO[126].

I did almost all things my uplines told me to do, system told me to do.
I devised all kinds of clever ways to contact people that most network marketers would never think of, let alone try. (Some of them are just embarrassing to share)

When I used to ask my uplines, why it is not working for me, they used to either tell me that "**You just need to do more of it**" or "**It's just a numbers game.**" or "**You just need to show more plans.**" and no matter how hard I tried, everything just turned out to be a utter disaster for me.

"If you are failing at something, it means only two things either you are doing something wrong or you are not doing something enough."

Some of my crosslines who were "**successful**" in the eyes of the society used to make me feel embarrassed in front of everybody asking me about "**How much money I was making?**" and although I was showing a lot of plans than 95% of the crowd, I had no results to show.

And after trying different things quite unsuccessfully, slowly and relentlessly, I proved to myself that no matter how I attempted to do this, it wasn't going to work the way my upline told me to do or system told me to do.

As I saw heavy duty attrition rate in system itself. People with 6 months & younger occupied 70% of seats. People with 12 months or less occupied 90% and remaining seats were occupied by people who were more than 12 moths.

Every month of coffee shop, travelling expense in that business became a bigger ball and chain of failure, mounting evidence of my ineffectiveness that eventually became impossible to ignore.

Agony-----Pain------Extreme Brokeness

I laboured under a burden of inner agony, maddening frustration and desperation. I wondered to myself how anybody could possibly explain or justify such a long, uninterrupted string of failure.

My greatest fear was that the prospect at my next meeting would ask me how much money I was making. I developed elaborate mechanisms in my presentations, just to prevent this question from ever getting asked and I learned exclusive methods to deflect that question skilfully.

"People want to succeed. They want to do a good job. They don't like to turn out lousy work. If your people are consistently failing, it's not their fault – it's your system's fault." W. Edwards Deming

Did that statement hit me like a ton of bricks?
No, not at the time.

Actually it slowly melted its way down through my brain like a hot steel ingot on a frozen lake. Every time they would tell us about how the system is flawless but still I could see most people quitting. I am not crying foul here. I don't have to.

Whenever they said

"We are the product of the system. The System is the secret, the system fails not."

I would look around and see the 99% failure rate and be reminded that someone must surely be jesting.

So I decided to keep aside the advice which was not serving me or most of the crowd anymore and I was determined to find answers on my own and this book is the result of those efforts I made.

When I started, we had no tools for making our life easier.
Only coffee shop meetings or home meetings. And mostly at the plush places, so the prospects coming there should get that higher class feel.

People were travelling from long places, driving long way to get to that coffee shop to show a single plan or meet his/her upline. Nobody complained about it. Even when that long mileage was piling up to become a huge stone of failure.

Some did continue despite seeing any long lasting results, most of them quit. Some never bothered to come only. They lost in translation.

For all my hard work, I had nothing to show for it but debt, an abundance of products and a dwindling list of friends who actually still talked with me.

The biggest epiphany I had is when I started dabbling and started learning about marketing, sales, copywriting, because I saw if I continue doing what I was doing for next 20 years... it's not going to give me any more results.

And I began looking for real answers to why I was spinning my wheels.
So I looked at the part which was not working and when I did, my entire view of this business changed forever.

I have written this book because I don't want everyone else to suffer just because they don't have the effective methods of prospecting.

2

Truth about Prospecting Methods

Does the same method of prospecting ever work for everybody?

Not at all.

There are lot of other methods to locate and create prospects. And all of the methods work – if you learn how to use the method correctly.

Why every single method of prospecting doesn't work for everybody?

Because everybody comes from different background, different life experiences, different education, different work experience and different strengths and different personality traits.

You should choose those methods which fits in with your personality and works the best for you. Also make sure you are comfortable doing it for a long time.

e.g. If you are using cold-calling to prospects and trying to set up appointments and every single day for last 3 months, you find it's dreadful and most humiliating experience in your entire life, then probably that approach is not the best for you.

But despite that there are many approaches you can test and see how well they work for you.

Many times you hear distributors say:
"Advertising doesn't work."
But is this true?
Of course not. We know advertising does work. If not, who is paying for all those people who do Facebook campaigns? What the distributor should be saying is:

"My advertising doesn't work."
Once the distributor takes that personal responsibility, prospecting starts to make sense. If a distributor's advertising doesn't work, then the distributor has two choices:

1. Invest the time and money to learn how to make advertising/ marketing work so that you can compete successfully with other advertisers/marketers.
or
2. If you don't want to invest anything, then simply choose a different method of prospecting.

Remember, you either have to invest time or money or both. Free prospecting methods are plenty but they involve more time and energy.

Each prospecting method is <u>not created equal</u>. Some methods are more powerful than others while some methods will work more powerfully with others, while some won't.

You shouldn't discount any method just because it's not working for you.

You'll hear distributors say:

1. "Cold calls don't work."
2. "Opportunity meetings don't work."
3. "Referrals don't work."
4. "Postcards don't work."

And the same truth applies to all of these methods of prospecting.
Distributors must find a method of prospecting that they enjoy, and then learn how to use that method – or pick another method.

This book has plenty of methods and resources for prospecting. You won't like them all.

Some won't apply to your business or personality.

But the important thing is to find at least one method that you can do and then go out and build a powerful downline organization.

Let's get started

3

How to Approach Friends and Family even complete strangers without resistance and Get over Rejection by never pitching them your MLM deal?

Rocket Recruiting App

You can use this app with your friends and family and even strangers without having to fear about getting rejected.

What's the best thing about this app is you don't have to lead with your MLM deal or Product.

It comes up with opportunity to save their monthly and yearly taxes by investing in your MLM business, so it's a sneaky approach.

If you happen to show them how you can help them in saving their taxes through this app and tell them how they can use that money in to invest into a home based business or MLM to get that benefit.

I am going to show you how to help your friends and family saving their hard earned money in taxes and earning at the same time.

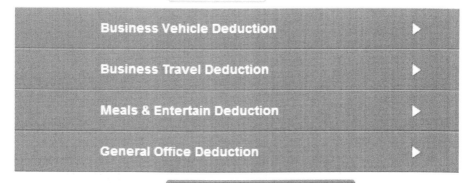

After you fill this, you will see this screen

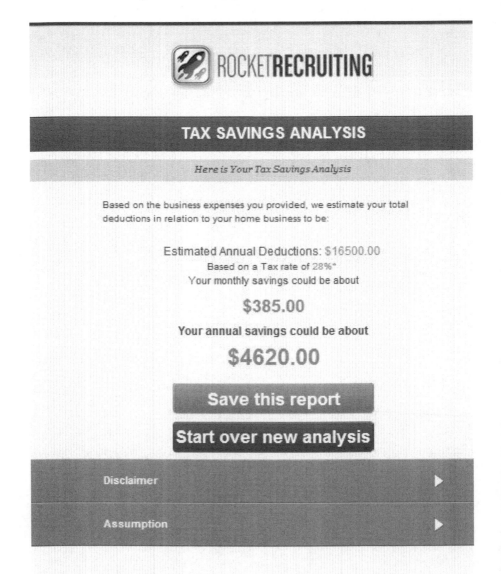

You can see the assumptions made to create this report after you click on "save this report"

You will see this screen

Save & Send Report

Fill the details about this contact

Full Name

Email Address

Mobile Number

Notes

Followup Date

Save & Email

Change the email format inside this

SEND REPORT BY EMAIL

Edit the Email text below before you send it.

Hi ████,

It was a pleasure talking with you today. You will find your Tax Savings Analysis attached.

Included in the pdf is a bonus, a special report called The Two Tax Systems. It's only two pages long, but the information it contains is important and not many people know about it. I know that you will find it useful.

I look forward to talking with you again soon.

All the best,

████

Path: p

Send Email

You will get mail along with attached PDF file

Hi █████

It was a pleasure talking with you today. You will find your Tax

Included in the pdf is a bonus, a special report called The Two know that you will find it useful.

I look forward to talking with you again soon.

All the best,

████████

Estimated Annual Deductions: $16500.00

Based on a Tax rate of: 28%

Your monthly savings could be about: $385.00

Your annual savings could be about: $4620.00

1597_2278_repor...

Richard Williams

Inside the report, you will find table like this

The Home Business Tax Savings Estimator will give you a good idea on how much you may save on taxes each year.

CATEGORIES		MONTHLY	ANNUAL
Home Office Deduction - home based deductions are available when any dwelling unit of yours is used on a regular basis for your business.	Total of any of the following: Mortgage, Rent, Real Estate Taxes, Monthly Utilities and Services, Mortgage or Renters Insurance:	$1,000.00	$12,000.00
Business Vehicle Deduction - use of any vehicle in the course of operating your home business may be deductible as a business expense.	Estimated number of miles driven monthly:	833.33	10,000.00
Business Travel Deduction - travel expenses incurred when business activity requires you to stay away from the principal place of business can be deductable.	Estimated cost of any of the following: Airfare, Hotel, Parking, and other related business travel expenses:	$166.67	$2,000.00
Meals & Entertainment Deduction - expenses incurred for meals and entertainment can be deductible if related or associated with your business.	Estimated cost of meals for the month: Any meals that were prepared and paid for outside of the home.	$500.00	$6,000.00
General Office Expense Deduction - general business expenses such as telephone & internet use, supplies and marketing materials may be deductible.	Estimated monthly cost of the following: Cell Phone, Internet, Office Phone, Gifts.	$300.00	$3,600.00
Your Total Monthly Expenses		2,800.00	
Your Total Annual Expenses		33,600.00	
ESTIMATED MONTHLY TAX SAVINGS*		**$385.00**	
ESTIMATED ANNUAL TAX SAVINGS*		**$4,620.00**	

18

4

How to Get paid for Prospecting and Make Money even when Nobody joins your Team ?

After you use Rocket Recruiting System, it's now time to generate targeted prospects through funded proposal.
It has many built in features.

1. Capture Page
2. Built in Lead Management System
3. Phone Scripts
4. Educational Videos
5. Affiliate Tracking

MLM brilliance
http://www.promarketingsystem.net/BrilliantHome.aspx

30-Day FREE Trial Request Form

☑ **YES!** I'll take you up on your generous 30-Day 'Full Access' FREE Trial. I get to use all the cool features of MLM Brilliance to superboost my business growth over the next month. If I'm not satisfied in any way I can cancel and owe nothing.

Once I see how powerful this recruiting system is I can continue to use it and will be billed on day 31.

However, with your Get 3 Get It FREE Promo I can continue to get it FREE. SO I've got nothing to lose - and a whole lot to gain.

There's NO long-term contracts. NO termination fee. I can cancel at any time. Count me in.

Choose any membership according to your preference
Their capture page

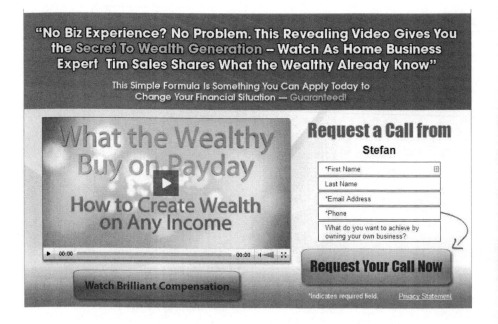

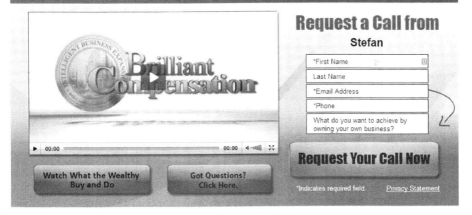

FAQ

Who sells the products?

In any business, products or services are sold — but how does it work in Network Marketing? Don't worry, the door-to-door days are long gone. Discover the 3 ways products are sold. This efficient model goes beyond traditional retail and has CEOs of the Fortune 200 taking notice.

Do I need sales experience?

The answer to this question surprises a lot of people. You 'recommend' every day without even realizing it. You'll soon learn 2 other ways sales ability happens in Network Marketing and neither of them involve you.

Do levels of commissions raise the price of the products?

When you know how traditional marketing and distribution happen the answer will be self-evident. With the Network Marketing model, product quality and innovation can increase dramatically without increasing the retail price to the consumer. This video shows why this happens.

Concerned about marketing to friends?

Stranger or friend, products are sold every day through these channels. Network Marketing is no different. You'd be surprised how many corporate deals happen with 'golfing buddies' out on the course. Listen in and see why this objection should be the least of your concerns.

Is it better to be hired by a company or sponsored into a network marketing company?

In today's corporate world the adversarial relationship between owners and employees has never been wider. Executives make big salaries and bonuses whether they succeed or fail — there's nothing fair about the system. Network Marketing has a system that's inherently fair since your success is tied directly to your sponsor's success. Watch the video to see what I mean.

5

Business Card Prospecting Technique

This is one of the unique ways of prospecting when you meet someone in person or you meet someone in networking meetings.

Most people don't pay attention to how they design their business cards. Here, I am not talking about designing most savvy, flashy and tasteful business cards. I am talking about designing cards where you can put call to action where they can take more information about you or your business and they are inside your follow-up funnel.

Check this example
www.perrymarshall.com

Why you need to create cards like this one?
Because if you tell people, you sell Skin Care Products or you

sell Gold Coins or even if you say you are a Home Business Consultant, even then people just don't care until you show them how it benefits them.

WIIFM: What's in it for me?

Instead your card says something which interests the potential prospect like a benefit statement

"I help working professionals to save upto $2000 taxes every year."

How many people now do you think will be interested in learning how to do that?

Quite a few.

But many of them have no idea what Home Business Consultant do and now when they ask "How do you do that?"

They have just opened the door for your offer.

Your business card should be "mini advertisement" of what you do.

FREE Report Reveals The Secrets Of Generating A Constant Flow Of New Clients, Patients, Or Customers Into Your Business!

- How To Generate A Constant Stream Of Qualified New Clients Who Are Calling You!
- How To Create And Implement Predictable, Reliable And Profitable Marketing Systems And Strategies!
- How To Create Systems To Automate Your Business So You Can Work Less And Play More!
- Marketing Techniques, Sales Letters, Ads, Flyers, And Other Proven And Tested Strategies That Will Cause Clients To Seek You Out!
- The Source Of Real-World Information And Success Secrets Designed To Build Your Business, Increase Your Income, And Live Your Life The Way You Want It!

Call The Toll-Free 24 Hour Recorded Message To Request Your FREE Report
(888) 000-0000

6

Postcard Recruiting Secrets

Postcard is one of the best ways to create interested local prospects, but before you dabble into it, you should know "IN"s and "OUT"s of it.

Why to use postcard?

1. Postcard doesn't need to be opened.
2. Postcards are short.
3. Printing and postage costs are cheaper.
4. Writing and designing is easier and less costly.
5. Postcard works for any business.

How to write a copy?
1. Motivating sequence

2. a. Get attention.
   b. Identify problem or need.
   c. Position your product/service as solution or answer.
   d. Prove your case.
   e. Tell reader what to do next.
   f. Give reader useful information. Don't fill it with fluff, hype and over-promise.

3. Attention Grabbing headline
   a. Be clear, direct and concise.
   b. The message should be reader centred.
   c. Highlight the product/service most important benefit.
   d. Arouse curiosity.
   e. Appeal to reader's self-interest.
   f. Don't overstate the benefits.
   g. Identify highly specific, extremely narrow target audience.
   h. Use meaningful specifics.
   i. Use odd no instead of even no.

4. Identify pain
   a. Interrupt conversation in prospect's head.
   b. Always write to a singular person.
   c. Be conversational.

5. Testimonials
   a. Testimonials should be powerful and should communicate specific benefits to the reader.
   b. Include pictures when possible.
   c. Don't make up your testimonials.
   d. Include any numeral or factual basics required.

6. List benefits
   a. People buy emotionally and justify logically.

7. Credentials
   a. Provide concrete credentials wherever possible.
   b. Use anecdotes and success stories.
   c. Don't let the credentials take the centre stage.

8. Anticipate objections
   a. Compare apples to oranges.
   b. Make the cost insignificant.
   c. Introduce one or two weaknesses.
   d. Never attempt to make prospect look silly, inept or uneducated.

9. Solution
   a. Reap the pain and emotional aspects.
   b. Present the solution as easy and effortless.
   c. Reveal the value before price of the actual product.
   d. Offer a free booklet or other bait piece.

10. Take away
    a. Make it unexpected.
    b. Use it as a tool of Reverse Psychology
    c. Paint a picture of how prospect can potentially lose out he/she doesn't sign up or purchase today.

11. Deadline
    a. Use limited time or limited quantity offers.
    b. Offer a discount for fast response and penalty for low response.
    c. Make deadline obvious.

12. Call to action
    a. Tell your prospect exactly what you want him to do.
    b. Supply atleast two response methods
    c. Provide sufficient incentive

13. Response Mechanism
    a. Phone no.
    b. Email id
    c. Website address

What's possible through postcards?

1. Retailing
Rent the local list of people who are amongst the target audience. Send them postcards and offer them a FREE trial.
Let's say 4 out of 100 responded. 3 agreed to use your product on trial. One purchased it after the trial.
You may not get much profit from the front end, but if you use this strategy to create 100 customers , then you have 100 people who bought your product, used it so you have 100 satisfied customers who can potentially become your next distributor.

2. Free Gifts and Certificates
Mail gift certificate to your existing customers.
Let's say $10 gift certificate. It will activate lot of old customers from your downline. Sure, you have to give $10 certificate but many more customers redeeming the certificate will order more than enough products to make it a profitable promotion.

3. Offer on your website
Use postcards to drive traffic towards your website, let them opt-in into contest, free gift or free drawing

4. Special Sale
Design a postcard something like this
Special Sale!! $200 off, your next vacation in Hawaii and Get Dinner at Mario's Italian Restaurant
People tend to give more response to Dinner offer than Discount.

Again, use what works for you. You don't have to be Rocket Scientist to do it.

7

How to Create a Lead Generation Tsunami through Blogging

This method can create frenzy of prospects coming to your website to become your distributors. To use this method, you must have a blog.

Tactic No. 1 : Define your target market. If you are in a company which sells health drinks, then your target audience is someone who might benefit from that drink. If you are a realtor, your target customer is someone who is going to buy real estate at an affordable rate. If you are a financial planner, then your customer is someone who is looking to invest his money in order to save his taxes and get greater returns. If your target is those people who want to start their home based business or those people who are already into home based business and want to succeed, then your target market is totally different.

Tactic No. 2 : How to persuade people to click on your link is done by writing simple message

Include P.S. at the end of every post, directing your prospects to opt-in for something which might help them or telling them to buy something (the product you have either used and chose to promote or something which you are affiliated with) Don't sell them on your opportunity yet.

You can use Rebel MLM as a funded proposal. www.amazon.com/dp/B00HHXKRYC

Tactic No. 3 : If you are not a technical person, you can get your WordPress blog setup from elance or odesk to save your precious time, use it only when you don't want to waste your time on learning something which might not be useful to you in the long term.

Tactic No. 4 : If you want to become content creation machine, then don't just become a consumer, always think like a marketer. Pay attention to all those things happening in your life. If you are going to an event, take notes, if you read some good book in your niche, take notes, if you do a mistake and learn a lesson, take notes and then write it on your blog.

Tactic No. 5 : The most important thing in blogging is consistency and congruency. Even if you suck at writing right now, but if you improve yourself day by day and you are congruent in your message, then in the long term nobody can beat you.

Tactic No. 6 : For proper Search Engine Optimization (SEO) of your blog, use these plugins : SEO Pressor(link here) and Easy WP SEO(link here)

<u>Tactic No. 7</u> : Become a member of <u>Betternetworker.com</u> and take paid membership and share your content there, it's a platform where more than 100,000 network marketers are registered and it's the best source of targeted traffic and leads. It's a really good platform for Content Syndication.

<u>Tactic No 8</u> : To build a list of eager prospects, you need to install these few plugins on your website. Premium List Magnet(link here), Popup Domination(link here)

If you want to learn more advanced stuff, Step by step strategies to build a blog from scratch, how to create content from scratch, how to get massive traffic to your website, how to convert your traffic along with email marketing strategies.

Go here
<u>www.rebelmlm.com/problogacademy</u>

How to create flood of prospects ?
Using powerful lead magnet.
Examples of powerful lead magnet
You can either create a report on your own or you can use this book to distribute, only make sure, you don't delete the information provided.

You can distribute as many copies you want. (If you have purchased the book, then you hold 100% re-sell rights)

But creating your report is the ultimate way.

1. 3 Questions to Close Prospects who are fence sitters

2. 6 low-cost high quality local lead generation strategies

3. How to create Hot prospects in Cold Market without any rejection

Now don't exactly copy and paste this but use it as a guideline. Make sure don't make it too generic like "How to sponsor more reps?" "How to find new prospects internationally?" and also don't create a lead magnet which doesn't solve immediate problem. Don't aim for long term solutions. Nobody likes long term solutions.

After they have opted in, create an auto-responder sequence which sends them email regularly until they sign up with you/ decided to talk with you or opt-out.

Few tips for creating auto-responder sequence
1. In 1st 2 mails, give away massive value; don't try to sell them anything.

2. Atleast use 15 mail sequences.

3. Use your photo, signature, mobile no., social profile at the end of each mail.

4. Direct them to content on your website, give them chance to direct them to your contact form page where they can leave their details and you can talk with them.

5. Build anticipation in each mail so their curiosity is building and open rate, click through rate is higher.

If you really want to learn the art of email autoresponder, I will suggest you to buy it

www.autorespondermadness.com

You can start selling funded proposal system to create qualified prospects.

You can start advertising your FREE Report through PPC, Press Releases.

Press Release will create floods of traffic to your report and it will eventually create lead generation tsunami.

Use new form of facebook advertising to laser target people in MLM market.

www.fbadtriad.com

Also the report is not limited to MLM.

You can also create a report around the major problem your product solves and write a report on

"How to Solve/Get rid of XXXXXX in YYYYY without ZZZZZZ?"
In that FREE report, write description of the problem, dangers of not solving it, conventional methods of solving it, introduce how to solve problem using method which involves

your product and in the end give your information, website information and strong call to action.

The basic principle behind this is Pre-selling your Products/ Service/Business Opportunity.

Unless you use strong call to action, the report is not of much use.
Use call to action something like this
Call Now and Get 3 FREE samples or Call now and GET a FREE Demo.

8

How to recruit people who are pitching you?

There are great deal of people who will try to pitch you online and offline.

Don't you get annoyed by them?

If you find someone is trying to pitch you, then don't avoid him/her because if you master this art, you will never have problem with them.

And the best part is they have no objections about MLM industry and they are not trained properly, so they try to pitch everybody within 3 feet of them.

1. The people who do this have no knowledge of how to market, so they pitch over and over again. Now I am going to suggest you tactic to sign up these people.

    Now understand, there are two types of people who pitch you, most people don't know how to market and that's why they pitch and very few people are really arrogant, they spam, harass others, you don't want to talk to these people, they are really close minded.

2. Some people are not trained properly by their upline or company and if you try to help them, it will actually

help you indircctly because they will have trust in you. Try to help them. Send them to your FREE reports, articles or any material which is not company specific.

3. The critical mistake people do when they bash others company, if you want to sign someone up from other company and if you start bashing his/her company, there is literally no chance for you to sign them up.

4. If they bash your company, then instead of backlashing on them, handle those with care, don't take it personally, remember you are helping them, don't lose your temper. If they seem like non-coachable, respectfully stop having conversation with them.

5. Find out their problem and tell them that you can offer them some coaching. Now it might happen that some people will take a lot of your time, you can send them a report or article, what it will do is, it will create trust factor that even if you are not in the same company but still you are helping them.

6. Try to be in touch with them. Don't overly empathize with them. Try to find out more about them their company and problems they are facing.

7. Give them indirect suggestions to be in your team. Let's say
   if you find out that someone is not getting required support from their uplines and he tells you the same. You should not directly tell him that don't worry, join my team, I will be a great support, instead tell him that "why don't you be with the team which is great

support?"

8. If you observe that they are not going to be a part of
   your team ever or it might take a long time, you can
   always direct them to relevant affiliate offers.

   a. Blackbelt Recruiting

   b. Pro Blog Academy

9

Additional Resources

Rebel MLM
www.amazon.com/dp/B00HHXKRYC

How to Become MLM Closing Monster ?
http://www.amazon.com/dp/B00JJ3UGVW

How to Double,Triple even Quadruple your Closing Ratio practically Overnight ?
http://www.amazon.com/dp/B00JIV3M48

Blackbelt Recruiting
www.rebelmlm.com/bbr

Rocket Recruiting
www.rebelmlm.com/rocketrecruiting

Postcard Recruiting
www.magicofmentoring.com
www.mlmmastery.com

Pro Blog Academy
www.rebelmlm.com/problogacademy

10K Social Media Recruiting
http://jessicahigdon.com/10ksocialmedia/

Printed in Great Britain
by Amazon